Picket Fence Signs

Hayley B Halliwell

Created with Vellum

For my best friend, Abbie.

Preface

In May of 2024, I hosted a writing challenge on social media. I posted a different random word every day, encouraging anyone doing the challenge to write a poem inspired by that word prompt.

I also did the challenge, but didn't truly dive in until August. By that time, with everything going on in the world, the challenge became something more for me.

The words that poured out of me were inspired by current events and topics leading into this year's election. And I knew that my heart was telling me I needed to keep that theme for the entire collection.

Each poem's title is the random word for the day, with the exception of the very first poem. And they are in order of when the word was posted on my social media.

Preface

I'm very proud of this collection. And I'm so excited to share it with those of you who I know will appreciate it.

1

Picket Fence Signs

Little girls making picket signs
using wood from picket fences,
using black paint on white posters
to scream without
using their voices.
Because no one listens
when they speak.

Not really.

Marching with signs,
paint still wet,
dripping down the posts
and to their skin,
droplets that match the tears
across their faces.
Tears of strength
this time around.
Because crying never

made a difference before.

Not really.

Picket signs made from
the posts of the fancy house's
white picket fence,
carried by little girls who are tired
of seeing so much of their future
in the clutches of destruction,
doing whatever they can to make
even a little bit of a difference,
waving cries for
change and awareness
in the faces of those
whose opinions matter,
as if there are lives
that depend on it,
because there absolutely are.

Really.

2

Remarkable

Facts presented on a platter,

trimmed with evidence

and quotes, coming not from

word of mouth or ear to ear,

but as bellows from recordings

taken from the very rooms

in which the person

stood there speaking it.

Images, with color and time stamps

and data showing the location

they were taken and the very

device that snapped the moment,

and often even the owner whose

hand that device was resting in

when every image was captured.

It's remarkable how much

proof is out there,

cast out as fiction in favor

of the lies fed by the people

who benefit most

from the hurt those lies cause us.

And yet so many keep digging in,

like they can't see the maggots

in the pie on their spoon.

3

Chain

They try to chain us to our yards,

like troublesome dogs they

don't know how else to deal with.

If they let us go, we'll go against them.

If they teach us to do good,

we'll go against them harder.

They do their best to train us

to do their dirty bidding,

but not all of us can be trained.

So they do what they can

to keep us chained.

4
Plaster

Your fist went through her emotions

the same way she watched it

go through the plaster

in the kitchen wall.

But you never touched her,

so it wasn't abuse.

Your words broke her down

the same way she watched

you break her stuff when

she got home a few minutes late.

. . .

Picket Fence Signs

But you never touched her,

so it wasn't abuse.

You cut her down to her lowest piece,

the same way you cut

all her ties outside of you,

making sure she had no one

to take her in, no way to escape.

But you never touched her,

so it wasn't abuse.

You reminded her that you

were the best part of her.

You told her she couldn't

survive without you.

You drilled it into her mind so deep

that she was lost when you left her,

oblivious to the fact that,

. . .

even though you never touched her,

it really was abuse.

5
Half

There isn't a day without

a devastating news article anymore.

I'm not sure there ever was,

but it's never been so

"in your face" as it is today.

Notifications on our phones

from news apps and social media sites

telling of weather destruction like

we've haven't seen in a lifetime,

terrorism, foreign and domestic,

Native American people

being murdered and abducted,

another school shooting,

and another, and another,

hate crimes happening across the US

without a lick of shame,

bad cops and bad parents

and bad government officials

and a bad fucking taste in

my mouth over all of it.

Half the time, I don't even want

to look at the news anymore.

But I won't be part of the problem

by pretending that there isn't one.

6
Truck

I used to hitchhike.

My feet were my only means

of transportation and, on occasion,

I would accept rides from strangers

who pulled over to offer.

I always thought I had good judgment.

I wouldn't accept a ride from someone

who gave off bad vibes, you know?

But I was also young and dumb

and thought I knew better than I did.

Most of the strangers were chill.

They picked me up and dropped me off

and I never saw them again.

But a few of the strangers...

were not so chill.

One of them showed up at

the night club I waitressed at.

He showed up couple times, actually.

One of them started asking questions

that were more than suspicious.

He honestly made me feel like that

ride was more of a close call

than it should've been.

But the older stranger who

made me stop hitchhiking,

the one who made me realize how

dangerous this all really was...

never even gave me a ride.

. . .

Picket Fence Signs

I was 19 or 20,

and almost to where I was going

when he pulled his

giant truck up next to me.

I didn't stop walking when he asked

if I needed a ride.

I pointed to the restaurant

directly ahead and told him

I was almost where I needed to go,

and also mentioned that

my boyfriend was waiting.

And I kept walking.

He pulled forward again,

a little in my way, and asked

if I was sure that I didn't want a ride.

I said again that I was almost there,

and added this time

that I was mad at my boyfriend

and anxious to speak with him.

And I walked a little faster.

He pulled up,

farther in front of me still,

and asked again.

But this time he asked if I wanted

to ride *him* rather than his truck.

"Are you sure you don't want

to give him something

to be jealous about?"

My "no" was cold, like the chill

his words ran down my spine.

He laughed and played it off,

"Hey, just thought I'd try!"

Like he hadn't just basically

backed a young girl into a corner

and kept asking for some kind of ride.

. . .

Picket Fence Signs

He pulled away for real this time,

leaving me to run the rest of the way

to the restaurant as soon as

he was out of my sight,

too afraid to walk back home for hours.

I stopped hitchhiking after that.

7

Justification

You hold your sign with your heart,

as you scream hate at those passing by,

people whose stories

you know nothing about,

but who dare to enter a place so evil.

Are they going in to have their child

ripped out of their God-given womb?

If they're going into this building,

then, honestly, what else

could you assume?

But most of the buildings

under that name

don't even offer what your

signs like to shame.

Most of the people going

through those doors,

aren't there for anything

but an annual checkup

or birth control, or free condoms,

or any of the other affordable

health benefits they offer.

Yet, still, you stand outside

and raise your signs and yell insults

you claim to be coming from love,

at victims of sexual assault who are

going in for Plan B so that they

don't have a pregnancy to abort later,

because they don't know if they'd

survive the mental toll it would take;

and the disabled person who would love

to have kids but knows their body

cannot survive a pregnancy,

that it would kill them both,

so needs birth control

to have the sex life that they

absolutely deserve to have;

and women who desperately

want to be moms,

whose bodies keep miscarrying,

and they just need the D&C

to keep the baby they wanted

but couldn't give life,

from staying in their womb

and either destroying

their chance to try again

or killing them.

You raise your sign,

painted with words of

murder and killer and pro-life hate,

yelling at people who are

likely only there for a pap smear,

maybe even their very first one,

and you use love as justification.

8
Discussion

It's funny how we used to be so close.

I could go to you for anything,

could talk to you for hours.

I always thought we had

so much in common,

that we were more alike than

I was to maybe even mom.

I always thought you were so mature,

that some of the things I had been told

about the way you had behaved

in your past just couldn't be true.

But then... things changed.

Picket Fence Signs

. . .

Even before I truly grew up,

you started showing me who

you really might be,

finding any opportunity to leave

political comments on my social posts,

even if the post was unrelated.

You started slowly making it obvious

that our differences in politics

meant more to you than

the things we had in common,

the things we used to

talk about for hours...

I stopped posting anything

that might be construed

as politically leaning.

I stopped sharing anything of the same.

. . .

I even stopped reacting in any way to
posts from friends, for fear you might
bring your comments to them,
since you so clearly wanted
to debate me, to change my mind,
even though I so clearly
had no reciprocation or intention.

I finally sent you a message.
Carefully worded.
As caring but clear as I could be.
Simply asking you to stop,
and even telling you it was hurting me,
and causing me anxiety,
and causing me to fear posting things.

And instead of having
a discussion with me,
you told me to block you.
And then blocked me first, instead.

. . .

Picket Fence Signs

The shock was instant, the pain raw.

I bawled, heaving sobs,

soul-crushing cries,

knowing that someone I loved so much,

loved politics more than they loved me.

9
Reasonable

I was only four years old

the first time I was backed into a corner

and forced by a boy to French kiss.

And after, when I spit in my

play-house plastic sink,

and said “eww” to the taste

of his hot, sour tongue,

he stared down at my

little form and told me,

“That's because you didn't do it right.”

As if a four year old should know

how to French kiss.

. . .

Picket Fence Signs

When a family member – by marriage,

at least – put his hand up my skirt

to rest on my thigh,

so close to my vulva that I could

feel the tremble of his fingers

even as my preteen body stiffened...

I was too scared to tell my mother.

Not because I thought

she might not believe me.

But because I was afraid I would

ruin a marriage if it turned out

he hadn't meant anything by it,

especially when I was so confused

how he could ever do that to me.

They divorced a few

years later, anyway.

I lost my virginity when I was drunk.

I was only fourteen and had

a crush on an older friend.

I had drink after drink, and we ended

up alone, in a room, in a bed.

He asked me over and over if I

was sure I wanted to do it.

And I said "yes", even giving him

a condom I'd kept in my purse.

I guess it's lucky that

someone interrupted,

because he told me a few weeks later

that he never even used it.

I was raped, drunk and alone

with a guy I had only just met,

my face shoved into

the corner of a couch

as he moved the lower half of my body

around and into a useful position,

my pants and underwear pulled down

just enough so that

he could do his business,

my fearful, drunken slurs of

"I'm going to go to sleep" ignored,

and his condom left out in the open

for my friends to find the next day.

I was too afraid to tell him no,

this man who was bigger than me

and who had already said

he was in the military.

I was left alone with him

and I was afraid.

I was way past the point of consent

had I even wanted to – which I didn't.

And I was also too ashamed,

when my friends found the evidence,

to tell them what really happened.

But the real slap in the face was

the phone call the next day.

"I bet you didn't think

you'd hear from me," he said.

As if he was covering his tracks.

. . .

College brought an abusive boyfriend

who used sex as a weapon.

And the first man I slept with after him,

was manipulative, even and

especially in the bedroom.

One man even tried so hard

to get anal sex from me,

that I had to put my feet on his chest

and push him away

when “no” wasn't enough.

Looking at my past, knowing the bullets

I've dodged and the

ones that didn't miss,

it's reasonable to me that most

women would choose the bear.

I know I would.

Because even knowing that

the bear might kill me,

I've never been raped by a bear.

10
Reservations

I don't want to be your

traditional wife

serving life

to a husband who just wants

a trophy by his side.

No, I won't stay home

and give you children

instead of giving

me my dreams.

You want a maid?

Hire one.

You want a nanny?

Do the same.

You want an obedient submissive

who only wants to give you

pleasure at the end of the day?

You'd be better off finding

someone who does it for pay.

No, I won't be your perfect little bride.

I won't be your brood mare,

and I won't keep your

alpha male dream alive.

I'm not here to serve you,

and I'm not here to follow your rules.

I wasn't made to play second fiddle.

and I don't need to borrow your tools.

So don't expect me to

cater to your image,

like you think all women should do.

Some of us like self-autonomy,

and recognize your brand of abuse.

11
Perfect

I tell my husband that our forever

home needs to have one of

those really big showers.

You know, the kind that has the

waterfall shower head

and the huge stone seat

already built in.

My husband says the

thing he really wants,

is an enclosed porch

that we can relax on,

something we can

feel the breeze through

without having to deal

with all the bugs, right?

And that would be perfect

for me to do some

reading and writing on

when I need a change of scene.

We don't need a mansion.

It doesn't even have to be

two stories, honestly,

especially with my chronic pain.

Though, a basement is a must for me

and my midwest anxiety.

We don't need a huge yard,

but something big enough

for a fire pit and washers

and maybe a dog.

Our dream forever home

doesn't need to be anything

super fancy or big or special.

But unfortunately, in today's economy,

our dream forever home

will likely always just be a dream.

12
Suffice

We're not trying to take

your fucking guns.

No one wants to take

your fucking guns.

But people like me, should not

be able to go out and buy one.

No, I am not a danger to anyone

outside of, maybe, myself.

No, I would never use a gun in

any way that would put

someone's life in danger.

I know how to use one,

and I know how to be safe with it.

But I should not be allowed to

walk in and buy a gun.

Not when I rely on antidepressants

to keep my chronic depression at bay.

Not when I have a history of

suicidal thoughts and ideations,

a history I'm still recovering from.

There should be absolutely zero reason

someone with mental illness like mine

can walk into a gun shop

and back out with a gun,

let alone in the same day.

And there ARE places

where that's possible.

Even worse, we see it all the time,

with people who are more than suicidal.

Picket Fence Signs

People who are murderous.

People who are both.

People who are using these weapons

in classrooms, on our children

and their twenty year old teachers.

People who are the very reason

kids are going to school and learning

Active Shooter Drills like it's

as normal as two plus three.

It shouldn't be so easy for people

who shouldn't have guns to get them.

Give us something to make it harder!

Longer holds before it leaves the store.

An exam to show you understand

how to keep it held

safely in your home.

Mental health checks.

Criminal backgrounds.

Not just once, but with an ID card

and a renewal, the same way

I have to do for the insurance that

would pay for my hospital bills

if someone came in

and shot up my work.

And yeah... maybe you also don't need

that shit-your-pants,

automatic boom banger

you like to show off to your buddies

on the weekends at the lake.

But right now, we really want

to make it harder for the people

who would be dangerous with a gun

to get their hands on one.

I think that would suffice to start.

So unless you're someone who

wouldn't pass a mental health check,

a criminal background check,

or a gun safety exam...

what the fuck do you

have to worry about?

13
Shaking

Sometimes I have to stop and question

if I'm shaking from frustration

or if I'm shaking from the pain.

They so often wake together

in my fragile, resilient body,

doing dances to forlorn

music on my heart.

Frustration over the pain.

Pain present for just existing.

Frustration over the

lack of understanding

from the people who see my smile

and don't believe it's masking a thing.

Sometimes I'm shaking from the pain.

Lately...

the frustration keeps me shaking.

14
Watching

We've grown up watching

crisis after tragedy after

world-altering event,

and people ask why millennials

have such a dark sense of humor.

If we don't make light of this one,

then the next big event might break us.

Of course, I say that like we haven't

seen so much that we aren't

a literal meme or conversation point.

Don't worry about the millennials,

this is the 7th or 8th time they've

dealt with something like this

in a single lifetime.

Oh? It's actually more than that?

Well... good thing we can

afford therapy, right?

Oh yeah, we can't.

Well, good thing for that

dark sense of humor, then, I guess.

I worry we wouldn't be able

to make it through the

next event without it.

15

Schedule

Some parents are buying

into the conspiracy theory nonsense,

regurgitating the bullshit they read

from websites without credibility

and doctors without a degree.

They eat up the fear mongering

like it's dessert for breakfast,

and dive down the rabbit hole

of misinformation head first.

And when they become an expert

on their new brand of ignorance,

they tend to brag about it

with their noses held up high.

Picket Fence Signs

They tell the whole world

that they didn't vaccinate their kids

for one reason or another

that never really makes much sense.

And while those parents are

defending their choices and carelessly

scheduling playdates with the town,

other parents are buying caskets,

and preparing to schedule funerals,

because their kids

couldn't be vaccinated,

and depended on others

being vaccinated instead.

16
Service

We're taught as children

to dial 9-1-1 in emergencies,

told that help will come.

And most of the time, that's true.

But it has been pointed out

time and time again that this

is not a service where

"most of the time" is okay.

There should never be an instance

where a trigger happy cop

kills an unarmed civilian.

There should never be a situation

where "I can't breathe" is ignored.

Picket Fence Signs

Why do we have cases

where people are dying

for seemingly no reason at all,

at the very hands of the people

who were there to protect them?

It shouldn't be so easy for

bad guys to get behind a badge.

And there definitely shouldn't

be so much protection

for those bad guys

when they take someone's life

and use that badge to justify it.

17

Music

We were so many steps ahead,

with flags flying more

prominently than ever,

rainbows splashed across

campaigns and merchandise,

"PRIDE" in all-caps on store windows.

Parades were popping up

in more and more cities,

music declared that we were

born like this and proud of it,

and pictures of couples

who weren't cis/het

showing off their rings

were filling our social medias.

And then the bigots got louder.

And louder, and louder,

until their shouts started

making movements.

Violence hidden behind

the loving hate of some religions,

snuffing out life in night clubs

and parks and bathrooms and city hall.

As if the Matthews and Harveys

and Brandons and Allens of our past

never made a difference.

But let me assure you, *they did.*

Love is stronger than hate

and being true to who you are

is bigger and braver than *anything*

those against us could

tuck into their holsters.

The bigots can spew their hate vomit

and pretend they don't remember

how far we've come or who

we lost along the way, but we know.

And we are proud to be a part of such

a beautiful community, where hate

doesn't have a letter in our title.

And whether we're out to everyone

or out to some, or out to no one

at all or even ourselves,

we're here and we're queer

and we will *never* stop fighting.

18
Refund

My intrusive thoughts

are getting louder.

They're saying things

I don't want to hear.

I won't lie or pretend

I've never had

intrusive thoughts

about suicide before.

But it's coming on more often

and it's scary.

I don't want to die. Ever.

That's the problem.

I'm uncomfortable with

the entire idea of death.

But my chronic pain,

and the lack of answers,

and the frustration

from the lack of answers,

and having to live life

like I'm not in agony

just from standing at the sink

for ten minutes

or trying to stay in

the shower long enough

to wash both my hair and my body...

The anger that builds

when the people around me

hear me talk about my pain

and even see me cry

when I can't hold it in,

and still don't believe I'm “that bad”

or even suffering at all.

When there are people resenting me

for needing accommodations,

like I *enjoy* needing things

modified for me.

It should be no surprise then,

with constant pain

and constant doubt around me,

that my intrusive thoughts have started

begging for a refund on life.

19
Offer

If I wear clothing that shows my skin,

I'm *clearly* doing it for attention.

Obviously, wearing short shorts

is scandalous and predatory,

even if there's a song from the 50s

declaring that women both

like and wear them.

The thin strip of skin you

see on my belly between

my ultra high-rise leggings

and the crop top I'm wearing,

must be meant to entice the menfolk.

Women don't wear certain clothes

because it's hot out and

they don't want to overheat.

They don't wear certain pieces

because they make them

feel good about themselves or

are simply comfortable.

We all know that women dress

themselves as an offer

to the men around them.

Because women *never* do things

for themselves, right?

There's always an agenda, right?

Or maybe...

Maybe women don't give a flying fuck

what people think

about what they wear.

And maybe they dress

however they want?

Because of the weather, or their mood,

or an event, or because they simply

like the damn outfit.

Maybe men have fuck all nothing to do

with a woman's choice in clothing

in most situations?

But what do I know?

I'm just a woman.

20
Goodnight

Working more of your week

than you spend living life,

to make a paycheck that

leaves you scrambling

to make it to the next payday,

is not a way to live.

When the majority of Americans

live on a minimum wage

averaging around nine dollars per hour,

and rent is over a thousand

dollars a month,

plus add in all the rest

of the bills and gas and food,

how do we expect Americans

to afford to live?

Homelessness is closer than

financial stability for so many people,

even with decent jobs

and excellent work ethics.

The country is working against us

and *for* the rich.

And still, so many can't see it.

They get ridiculous tax breaks,

but I can't afford physical therapy.

Politicians are buying second yachts,

but it took me five years to fill a cavity.

The rich can go to sleep without

having to worry if tomorrow will

be the day that they lose everything.

Because it won't be.

Would I like to be rich?

I wouldn't mind it.

But what I really want, more than

almost anything most days,

is to be able to kiss

my husband goodnight

without knowing that the cobwebs

in my bank account will be

twice as thick tomorrow.

21

Pressured

I am seven credits and a civil exam

away from having a college degree.

But that was fourteen years and

ten thousand dollars in debt ago.

I wouldn't have taken a student loan

if I had been able to think on my own.

But I was young and naive and

in an abusive relationship.

He berated and ridiculed me,

and threatened our future

if I didn't continue my education.

As if that was something he had

done for himself.

So I went to see an advisor and got,

not one, but two student loans.

“To equal what I would have gotten

from the FAFSA that semester.”

Loans totaling well above

the cost I needed for tuition.

Most of which, my abusive boyfriend

spent, rather than me.

I can't help but wonder,

if the student loan advisors

were trained to talk to students

about their situation in a safe space,

to notice when someone might be

being pressured to get them,

would I have gotten mine?

Or would I have dropped out

then like I wanted to?

If there had been someone trained,

not to sell me on a loan,

but to see below my surface,

would I have been protected?

22
Stuffing

"I do it because I love you,"

they say, as they remind you

you're going to hell simply for being

who you can't help that you are.

They fight to put commandments

in schools, saying it's a core value,

that it should be part of

regular education.

But they also fight like hell to keep

our kids from learning proper sex ed,

preferring instead that they stumble

into relationships not even knowing

how their own bodies work; or worse,

not understanding safe sex or consent.

"We need Jesus in the White House!"

they cry, with red cheers and tears

and arms held to the sky.

But ask to give

other beliefs a fair stage,

and you might as well be asking for

Witchcraft to be taught in schools.

Stuffing religion into our

classrooms and speeches and

public events is their goal,

but only if it's the right one.

And when we remind them of

Separation of Church and State,

they pull an excuse from their Bible

and turn the other way.

23

Math

People shouldn't have to

do the math to see if it's worth

going to the hospital,

or if it would cost less

to just die, instead.

Healthcare should be a right

without having debt attached.

People shouldn't be dying

of things that are treatable,

simply because they couldn't

afford to go to the doctor.

Illnesses shouldn't be

progressing beyond help,

because the fear of hospital debt

outweighs the fear of

that illness putting you in a casket.

That so many people have

been brainwashed by

the very companies who benefit,

brainwashed to believe

that universal healthcare

is worse than dying

or being in debt...

that *so many* believe these things

and actively vote against it,

is proof that the right

cares more about lining their pockets

than they care about any of

the very voters they've brainwashed.

24
Breathing

Seeing it so blatant and unashamed,

hearing them openly state it,

as if they've been one wrong situation

from bursting and are finally breathing

big, hateful breaths of white air...

watching them proudly wear

propaganda for their chosen idol

who not only made them feel like

it was safe to be open,

but is also endorsed by

proud children and those who hide

behind a white hood...

all because one awful man

stoked the fires of hate in their asses,

and merely smirked

when hate said *hello*.

When officials like to ignore evidence

and the pleas of a victim's family

not to execute a black man who

evidence says is innocent,

and he dies anyway...

when corrupt cops like to shoot first

and pretend not to be racist later...

when they'll kneel on the backs of

black men who can't breathe,

but spit at the feet of those who kneel

to bring awareness of these acts...

when people see #BlackLivesMatter

and clearly miss the fucking point when

they reply with #AllLivesMatter,

like we don't know that every life

is important when we're fighting

to keep the ones in danger alive...

But there are so many of us out here

trying to bring awareness

and be bigger than their hate.

And I know it's not my story to tell,

and I recognize my privilege.

And though my voice

might be little in the crowd,

I will stand, I will fight, and

I will shout for change with you.

25

Possible

I never thought it would be possible
to find myself alive during a time
when rich politicians are fighting
to take away our libraries.
Something that has been a staple
of communities for centuries,
knowledge from our past
and stories written to pass
along for generations.
Buildings that have evolved
from simple places that hold
archives of written material
for safe keeping and reading,

to hubs of culture and learning

and a place to find help

getting back on your feet.

Books and free internet and

a place to hang out when

it's too hot or too cold.

Computers and movies and events

for people of all ages to find

comfort and community and education.

Libraries today offer so much more

than most people ever realize.

And why, do you think,

would anyone want to take that away?

26

Student

Take away education,

and they won't be smart enough

to call you on your bullshit.

Keep them from learning about

the atrocities of our past,

and they won't know any better

when they learn the truth

about the men they think are heroes.

You feed them ignorance like candy

and hope your handiwork

does you favors.

But you never expected parents

to fill in the gaps you were taking out.

Picket Fence Signs

Try as hard as you want to change

the education our kids are receiving.

With or without our help,

they'll eventually catch on.

And they won't be a student

to your bullshit any longer.

27

Breakfast

You spend so much effort

making sure our country is

full of babies whose parents

are absent or poor or

practically babies themselves.

But when those babies

make it into this world,

you no longer seem to care.

Throw them into the system,

leave their parents without support,

and God forbid you pay a couple

dollars extra on your taxes

to make sure no child

goes without lunch at school.

You spit profanity at the idea

of paying a little more in taxes to

make sure no kid goes hungry,

some of those kids being the ones

you made sure would be alive.

And yet you can't be bothered

to help them stay fed,

actively fight against it,

as you sit there eating your

loaded omelet for breakfast,

while they stare at an empty tray.

28
Using

Another headline splashed across

our news feeds, with emotionless text

that somehow screams the words,

“Fentanyl OD”, like it's as normal

as announcing the losing score.

People using drugs to escape reality,

not knowing that this particular

fix has a little extra punch.

And that little extra is about as little

as a Greyhound looks by a kitten.

Dealers packing their product

with this extra shit,

not even telling their

customers what they're getting into,

handing over death

disguised as a fun time.

Purple stones popping up

across the world,

an army of broken hearted loved ones,

spreading awareness

and never backing down.

Because this is a fast moving crisis,

a quiet disaster,

leaving death in its path

and fiery craters in our hearts.

Craters that burn with grief and

an endless passion

to stop this madness.

To put an end to this crisis.

To save at least one life from

becoming another face

on a purple stone.

29
Wedding

How crazy are your morals

when you claim to be voting

in favor of the children,

and always doing what's best for them,

when you're making decisions that

literally put their lives in danger?

When right-wing officials would

rather see a child have

a wedding with her rapist,

than allow her to abort

the child he impregnated her with?

When people would rather force

more children into the system

for their "pro-life" beliefs,

and "saving the babies",

but the moment those babies

breathe their first breath of air,

they're on their own?

No help from the government.

No aid in the life they sometimes

weren't even wanted in.

No guarantee of a loving family

or even a pair of shoes that will fit.

But they slap themselves on the back

because another life was saved.

How is any of that pro

anything but ego?

They aren't pro-life

after the baby is born.

They aren't pro-life when

the mother's life is in danger.

They aren't pro-life when

the mother's mental health is

spiraling because of her situation.

They aren't pro-life when

the mother wants that baby

and will lose the ability to have

more if she can't have her

miscarriage attended to.

They aren't pro-life when

it's children having children,

or someone going back

to an abusive home,

or a health crisis that demands action.

You know? The longer I go on,

the less it seems like they're

really pro-life at all.

30
Know

The world is scary and growing

scarier by the day.

I'm lucky to have a partner

who understands,

who grew up raised by women

and instilled with the knowledge that

women aren't inferior to him by default.

I'm lucky to have a partner

who sees the way things are going

in our country right now,

and recognizes my fears

and even shares them.

I'm lucky to have a partner who,

when I asked if he

would get a vasectomy

with my life now being

considered secondary,

he didn't even have to question it.

"Yes," he said. "Of course."

I'm lucky to have a partner who,

when I asked if we'd

move to a safer state

if things here went as bad as they

looked to be headed,

his answer was almost immediate:

"I guess we'll have to."

I'm lucky to have *my* partner,

who loves me and cares for me,

and doesn't view me as

"a woman who can give him children",

but as his partner in life.

I'm lucky to have a partner

that I don't have to be afraid of.

Picket Fence Signs

That I know truly loves me

for who I am and not

what I can give him,

and who will always do his best

to keep me safe from

the rest of the world.

31
Count

Stories passed by word of mouth

and paintings on cave walls.

Inscriptions in stone tablets

and ink strokes across leather pages.

From notebooks to typewriters

to computers to phones,

writing words with a pencil

or a keyboard or our voice...

For as long as humans have been

able to tell stories, we've been

pouring creativity from our minds

in ever-evolving ways.

One thing, though, we didn't count on,

was technology evolving to allow

itself to do the writing for us.

Instead of us.

But don't you worry,

not a single, little bit.

The real writers will keep on writing.

We won't let generative AI do any

of the writing for us.

We don't need to.

No matter your background,

your financial situation,

your health, your age,

or anything else...

if you want to write a story,

all you need is your mind, your will,

and a way to get the story on

the screen or paper.

And if you choose to use

generative AI anyway?

Well, then I guess you didn't

really write anything

other than a prompt, did you?

32
Finish

You ban books like you throw

Black men into prison,

with calculated thought,

for your own benefit,

and often at no fault to them.

You tear stories from

the few libraries we have left,

having made the decision

that the context is too much.

Too controversial or vulgar

or right on the fucking nose

about things you don't want

us filling our brains with.

Knowledge is power

and power in the hands of the people

is much harder to deal with

than millions of those same people

forming picket lines and waving signs

outside of schools and libraries

and government buildings,

calling for change of stance

and change of leadership,

and to put a stop to censorship.

Nothing will change, I'm sure.

You'll never stop trying to dictate

what we read,

and we'll never stop

reading those books, anyway.

And while we're on the topic

of books you'd like to ban,

something tells me this one

will be on that list, too.

How to Make a Difference

- vote.gov
- thehotline.org
- blacklivesmatter.com
- thetrevorproject.org
- plannedparenthood.org
- ala.org/bbooks
- usa.gov/buying-home-programs
- 988lifeline.org
- 211.org
- needymeds.org
- samhsa.gov
- mayday.health
- https://www.facebook.com/groups/966990137888046

About the Author

Hayley B Halliwell is a queer author living in southern Missouri with her husband of over a decade, and their cat, Roswell Soup. When she isn't writing or working her day job, she can usually be found crocheting or playing video games. She is aware of the contrast between those two. Hayley is very open about living with mental illness and chronic pain, and hopes to break the stigma surrounding them.

- amazon.com/stores/Hayley-B-Halliwell/author/B0CKNVL38H?ref=ap_rdr&isDramIntegrated=true&shoppingPortalEnabled=true
- threads.net/@hayleybhalliwell
- facebook.com/hayleybhalliwell
- instagram.com/hayleybhalliwell
- patreon.com/HayleyBHaliwell
- tiktok.com/@TikTok.com@hayleybhalliwell

About the Cover Artist

Ali is an artist and illustrator based in the U.S., where she lives with her husband and children. She loves to create cozy illustrations that inspire hope and celebrate the simple joys of everyday life. Ali draws inspiration from nature, animals, vintage fashion, books, and her kids. When she's not creating art, she enjoys spending time with her family, reading, knitting, sewing, baking, and playing cozy games. You can find her art on Instagram and Threads, where she shares under the name @juniper.charm.

Milton Keynes UK
Ingram Content Group UK Ltd.
UKHW032039191024
449814UK00011B/643